STUDY GUIDE   SEVEN SESSIONS

FORGIVENESS!

THE KEY TO

EMOTIONAL FREEDOM

THE POWER OF LETTING GO

Graeme and Julia Cann

Forgiveness/The Key to Emotional Freedom Study Guide © Graeme & Julia Cann, 2025

All rights reserved. No part of this publication may be reproduced, stored in a retrieval system or transmitted in any form by any means, electronic, mechanical, photocopying, recording or otherwise, without the prior permission of the author — except in the case of brief quotation embodied in critical review and certain other non-commercial uses permitted by copyright law.

Cover picture source by G. Lewis. Used with permission.

Forgiveness! The Key to Emotional Freedom: The Power of Letting Go

1. Forgiveness. 2. Emotional Healing. I. Title.

ISBN: 978-1-76411-171-3

All scripture references (unless specified) from the New Living Translation (NLT) © 2004, 2007, 2013, 2015. Used with permission.

PUBLISHED BY GRAEME CANN

www.graemecann.com

TABLE OF CONTENTS

INTRODUCTION — page VI

WEEK 1 — page 8

Based on Chapters 1 & 2
WHAT THE BIBLE TEACHES ABOUT WOUNDS

WEEK 2 — page 12

Based on Chapters 3 & 4
THE WAY FORWARD

WEEK 3 — page 16

Based on Chapters 5 & 6
WHEN ARE WE READY?

WEEK 4 — page 22

Based on Chapters 7 & 8
FREQUENTLY ASKED QUESTIONS

WEEK 5 — page 26

Based on Chapters 9 & 10
PREPARING TO FORGIVE

WEEK 6 — page 32

Based on Chapter 11
THE STAGES OF FORGIVENESS

WEEK 7 — page 36

Based on Chapters 12-14
BIBLICAL FOUNDATIONS OF FORGIVENESS

INTRODUCTION

The reason we have written the book "Forgiveness! The Key To Emotional Freedom" and compiled this group study material is because we passionately believe that God's forgiveness of us, and our forgiveness of others, both sit at the very centre of the Gospel and are vital for the health and the unity of the Church.

Understanding and experiencing our salvation, our adoption into God's family, the fulness and power of the Holy Spirit and our mission as individual children of God and as the Church, is only possible through faith in the redemptive death and resurrection of our Lord Jesus Christ. And the only reason for such a sacrifice and such a powerful demonstration of God's love was His desire to offer absolute forgiveness to humankind.

Likewise, the message of His amazing grace is proclaimed to the world by His redeemed children reflecting His love, acceptance and forgiveness, by loving and forgiving our friends and our enemies as He has loved, accepted and forgiven us.

Our concern is that so many of God's children have an impoverished view of His grace, and so many churches are divided and disempowered by a failure to fully understand this biblical truth.

Hence this series of studies. Our prayer is that both you and your Church may be richly blessed by engaging in them.

WEEK ONE

What the Bible Teaches about Wounds

Based On Chapters 1 & 2

KEY MESSAGES

- The Main Reason To Forgive Those Who Hurt Us Is That Unresolved Anger Becomes Resentment And Resentment Damages Us And Our Relationships.

- Most Of Us During Our Lifetime Will Experience Hurt Of Some Type. There Are Three Main Sources Of Emotional Woundedness

    o The First Source Of Woundedness Is ... *The Damaging Behaviour Of A Perpetrator Or Significant Other.* (See Danny And Leila Abdalla's Story)

    o The Second Source Of Woundedness Is ... *The Damage Caused In Our Own Lives* ... Because Of Our Choice Not To Forgive. (See Graeme's, Alina's And Albert's Stories)

    o The Third Source Of Woundedness Is ... *The Hurt We Cause To Those We Love* ... Because We Refuse To Forgive The Person Who Hurt Us. (See Colin's story)

DISCUSSION

1. Have you ever yourself asked a similar question that Danny asked himself? *"Do I remain bitter and resentful and risk losing everything and every-one dear to me, or do I forgive and move on in order to live a fulfilled life?"* (1 John 4:7–21)

Forgiveness is sometimes difficult but is essential if we are to find the key to emotional freedom. If you need to forgive someone, what might make it a difficult thing to do? (Colossians 3:12–17)

----

2. Internalising painful emotions has the potential to damage our mental, physical and relational Health. Have you experienced this yourself? (Ephesians 4: 30–32)

----

3. As a group consider the two questions Graeme was asked by his counsellor. *"Do you believe that God, your Creator and Father freely offers you forgiveness for every sin you have committed, on the basis that Jesus Christ willingly suffered and died for each of them?"* (Rom 5:1–11)

and

"Do you believe that God, your Creator and Father freely offer forgiveness to every person who has ever hurt you.... on the basis of the death and resurrection of Jesus Christ?" (Matt 6:9–15)

[NOTE: We urge you to not gloss over these important questions.]

Week Two

The Way Forward

Based on Chapters 3 & 4

KEY MESSAGES

- Forgiveness is the only way to deal with resentment. Ephesians 4: 29–32 presents us with both a Statement of Goals and a Charter of Values. Here Paul challenges to forgive as we have been forgiven.
  Also read John 13:34; Rom 12:10; 15:5;
  1 Thess 4:18; 5:11; 1 Cor 12:25; Col 3:13.

- The compared perspectives of Secular and Christian on forgiveness.
  [Re-read them before discussing]

DISCUSSION

1. Discuss the book's definition of forgiveness:

   "We forgive another ... when we lay down our resentment and our desire for revenge ...

   and set the other person free from the obligation to suffer for the wrongs they have committed against us ...

   just as God has set us free from the obligation to suffer for the wrongs we have committed against Him."

   Do you agree that to forgive or not to forgive is a personal choice? (Luke 23–24). Why/why not?

   ----

2. Discuss the concept of Wounds and scars. Use the passage in John chapter 20 where Jesus shows his disciples his scars.

----

3. If God's forgiveness of us is a consequence of His love, and He has commanded us to love others as he has loved us, what might that look like for you? (1 Cor13: 1–7)

Week Three

When are we Ready?

Based on Chapters 5 & 6

KEY MESSAGES

- We are not always aware of our need to forgive. (Colin's story.) It is possible to live with emotional and relational injury without ever relating them to our internalised pain.

- Graeme and Julia share nine reasons why forgiveness is often rejected by those who carry long term resentment. These are:

    1. A misunderstanding of what true forgiveness is.

    2. A belief that it is unfair and unjust that the perpetrator receives forgiveness while the survivor continues to deal with the consequences of their actions.

    3. They believe that in some way maintaining their anger is a way of punishing the perpetrator.

    4. They do not understand the connection between their response to past hurts and the emotional and relational issues they are currently facing.

5. They do not realise that their bitterness and resentment are natural consequences of the hurt they suffered but are the consequence of their choice not to forgive.

6. Because they believe that the primary beneficiary of forgiveness is the one who receives it, forgiveness appears unfair.

7. They do not understand that their anger and resentment is negatively impacting their health and their relationships.

8. The hurtful event may have happened so long ago that they might not see the relevance of forgiveness.

9. They do not understand or obey the command in Colossians 3:12–13.

DISCUSSION

1. If forgiveness was a healing process that began when Colin realised how much his response to the event was negatively impacting him, then what might be the things that prompt us that it is time to forgive?

   ----

2. Read Colossians 3 12–13. Why do you think it is so difficult, as Jesus followers to choose to be merciful, kind and forgiving?

   ----

3. Discuss the three things we need to do before we forgive:

    1. Examine the consequences of holding on to anger.
    2. Become aware of how internalising negative emotions can and will affect you and your relationships.
    3. Release the mistaken belief that you must forget the hurtful event in order to forgive.

----

4. Study Matthew 5:3–12 together. Take note especially of verse seven.

NOTES

WEEK FOUR

Frequently Asked Questions

Based on Chapters 7 & 8

KEY MESSAGES

- **RESENTMENT:**

Resentment is a complex, multilayered emotional reaction to being mistreated or wronged by another person , situation or series of circumstances. When internalised it may be experienced as a merging of anger, bitterness, disgust, disappointment and disapproval.

- **SOME OF THE COMMON INDICATIONS THAT RESENTMENT IS IMPACTING OUR LIVES.**

Your negative emotions keep resurfacing. Anger becomes a perennial issue in relating to others. You can find no closure for the painful event. You may have feelings of regret and remorse or increasing feelings of anxiety and tendency toward emotional withdrawal.

- **DOES MY FORGIVENESS OF THE PERPERTRATOR PARDON THEM FOR THE WRONG THEY COMMITTED TOWARDS ME?**

No! forgiveness does not release the wrongdoer from their accountability, nor does it remove any obligations they have in relation to the law. At best when a person receives undeserved forgiveness, it may bring them to repentance for their wrongful behaviour, so opening the way for reconciliation.

- **WHAT DOES THE WORD REPENTANCE MEAN?**

Webster's Dictionary defines repentance this way: *'To feel sorry or self-reproachful for what one has done or failed to do. Be conscience stricken or contrite. To feel such regret or dissatisfaction over some action or intention as to change one's mind or behaviour. To feel so sorry for our wrongful behaviours that we change our ways. Be penitent.'*

DISCUSSION

1. Discuss all the questions in the list above and others included in the book.

   ----

2. Share personal stories about each one's forgiveness journeys including a time when someone has forgiven you.

   ----

3. In your group prayer-time, pray the Lord's Prayer together.

Week Five

Preparing to Forgive

Chapters 9 & 10

KEY MESSAGES

- The first preparatory step we need to take before we begin the process of forgiving the person who hurt us is to answer the question, '*What is the hurter responsible and not responsible for?*'

- In answering this question, it is always helpful to revisit the event and even tell your story to another. The reason this is important is ... that it helps us to recognise that the hurter is completely responsible for their actions. The blame belongs to them. Any shame we feel about the event also belongs to them.

- It is equally important that we accept responsibility for holding on to the anger and resentment. *Only we* can choose to give it up.

- Accepting responsibility for our emotional reactions and the hurtful behaviours that flow from them involves apologising to those we have hurt and asking for their forgiveness; and asking God for his forgiveness also.

- Corrie ten Boom, Nelson Mandela and Danny and Leila Abdallah are some of the great human examples of forgiveness.

DISCUSSION

1. Do you agree that if the two primary themes of the Bible are estrangement, and reconciliation, then forgiveness is the process that addresses both those themes?

---

2. As you discuss forgiveness ... what is the significance of the story of the prodigal son linked with the Lord's Prayer and Paul's teaching in Ephesians 4 and Colossians 3?

---

3. What is the real reason for forgiving a person I have been resentful toward?

---

4. Read Psalm 103 together. What verse or verses speak to each of you personally. Talk about it and read it each day until you meet again as a group.

NOTES

Week Six

The Stages of Forgiveness

Based on Chapter 11

KEY MESSAGES

In our work with people who have reached the point where they are willing to forgive and have prepared their heart to forgive there are several steps or stages that are helpful, some of which we have introduced earlier.

- **Step 1.** *Revisit the painful event.*

It is in revisiting the painful event and telling your story to someone as Graeme and Alex did, that we understand why it impacted us as it did. It helps us recognise that the shame we often carry is not ours but belongs to the wrong doer, and that the responsibility to open the prison doors is ours, not theirs.

- **Step 2.** *Seek forgiveness from others and from God.* (Cyril's story p88).

When we have carried resentment, it often expresses itself as anger, irritability, impatience, criticism, cynicism and sarcasm. These behaviours hurt the people we love. Our repentance and their forgiveness are important factors in our healing.

- **Step 3.** *Forgive the Person who has hurt you.*

This means that following the example our heavenly Father, we set our hurter free from the obligation to suffer at our hands, for what they have done to us.

- **You do not need to feel forgiving.**

You need to forgive out of gratitude. Feeling forgiving will always follow the act of forgiving.

- **Turn your tombstones into milestones.**

Memories of painful events, like tombstones, remind us of loss, grief and pain. On the other hand, milestones speak of how far we have come since the last one we passed.

The good news is that God has the power and the will to transform your tombstones into milestones and when He does ... every memory will become a memorial to your healing, rather than a reminder of your pain.

- Pray a prayer of confession and repentance. Ask for and receive God's forgiveness.

DISCUSSION

1. Read Psalm 51 together. The context is that this is David's prayer after being told by the prophet Nathan, that his sin with Bathsheba was known by God. Go through the Psalm and ask three questions.

- Where does the forgiveness of God come from?

- What did David ask for?

- What did David promise God? Discuss how all your answers relate to us.

WEEK SEVEN

Biblical Foundations of Forgiveness

CHAPTERS 12 – 14

KEY MESSAGES

- God blesses the merciful (Matt 5:7)

- Forgiveness is rarely deserved. (Matt 5:38–42)

- God commands us to forgive even our enemies. (Matt 5: 43–48)

- Our forgiveness of others must mirror God's forgiveness of us. (Matt 6:12)

- It is impossible to fully experience God's forgiveness if we do not forgive others in the same way. (Matt 6: 14–15)

- Jesus tells a powerful parable. (Matt 18: 21–35)

DISCUSSION

As we conclude our series, let's review what we have learnt by discussing the five main principles drawn from Jesus' teaching in the Gospel of Matthew, and Paul's teaching in Ephesians 4:25–32 and Colossians 3:12–15.

- The most damaging impact of a painful event rarely comes from the event itself.

- The emotional pain from our responses to an event cannot be resolved just by seeing justice done. Justice or punishment are never enough.

- Forgiveness is not given for the benefit of the wounder, but for the benefit of the wounded.

- Experiencing God's unlimited and unconditional forgiveness empowers us to forgive others in the same way.

- Jesus Christ has not only died for every wrong we have committed but also or every wrong committed against us by others.

NOTES

NOTES

www.ingramcontent.com/pod-product-compliance
Lightning Source LLC
Chambersburg PA
CBHW071918070526
44583CB00016B/2038